ANIMAL
ART

ANIMAL ART

Originally published as DRAW 50 ANIMALS

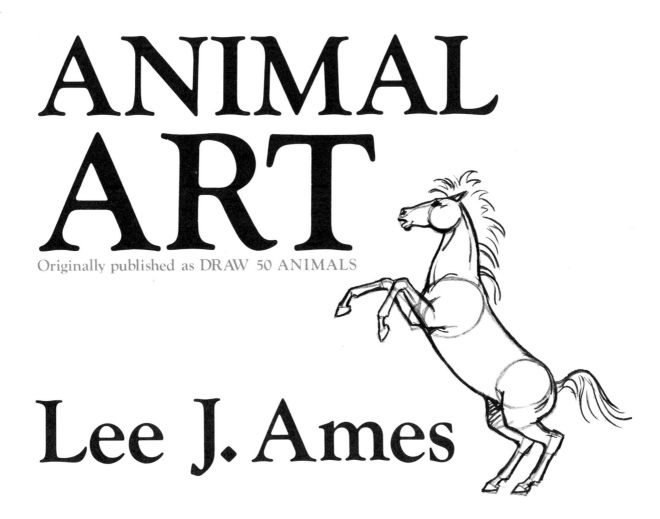

Lee J. Ames

Doubleday & Company, Inc.
Garden City, New York

ISBN 0-385-24227-1
Copyright © 1974 by Lee J. Ames
ALL RIGHTS RESERVED
PRINTED IN THE UNITED STATES OF AMERICA

To *Jocelyn, Alison, Jonathan,* and *Linda*

400 Ellinwood Way, Suite 300, P.O. Box 232008, Pleasant Hill, California 94523 • (415) 680-8697

Dear "Animal Artist":

Do you ever feel like you just "can't draw?" When you were smaller, you probably never thought about it, and certainly weren't really concerned what your picture would look like when you were through. You drew because drawing was fun. But you know, you are still just as creative as you were when you were five. And drawing is still fun! You CAN draw, and that's what this book is all about!

In this wonderful book, the author has given step-by-step directions about ways to draw many animals, teaching you the basic techniques and form relationships helpful to drawing them. Use this book as a starting point, and as you gain confidence look around and draw what you see in nature around you.

Sometimes when we think we can't do something, the only problem is that we have not yet learned to do it. Adults have the same problem with creativity, too! Once you decide to learn this skill, I think you may surprise yourself with how well you do! This book will help you learn the skill of drawing, and develop a talent that you can enjoy for the rest of your life. I wish you many many hours of happy drawing!

Best wishes,

Lane Nemeth
President

To the Reader

This book will show you a way to draw animals. You need not start with the first illustration. Choose whichever you wish. When you have decided, follow the step-by-step method shown. *Very lightly* and *carefully,* sketch out the step number one. However, this step, which is the easiest, should be done *most carefully.* Step number two is added right to step number one, also lightly and also very carefully. Step number three is sketched right on top of numbers one and two. Continue this way to the last step.

It may seem strange to ask you to be extra careful when you are drawing what seem to be the easiest first steps, but this is most important, for a careless mistake at the beginning may spoil the whole picture at the end. As you sketch out each step, watch the spaces between the lines, as well as the lines, and see that they are the same. After each step, you may want to lighten your work by pressing it with a kneaded eraser (available at art supply stores).

When you have finished, you may want to redo the final step in India ink with a fine brush or pen. When the ink is dry, use the kneaded eraser to clean off the pencil lines. The eraser will not affect the India ink.

Here are some suggestions: In the first few steps, even when all seems quite correct, you might do well to hold your work up to a mirror. Sometimes the mirror shows that you've twisted the drawing off to one side without being aware of it. At first you may find it difficult to draw the egg shapes, or ball shapes, or sausage shapes, or to just make the pencil go where you wish. Don't be discouraged. The more you practice, the more you will develop control.

The only equipment you'll need will be a medium or soft pencil, paper, the kneaded eraser, and, if you wish, a pen or brush.

The first steps in this book are shown darker than necessary so that they can be clearly seen. (Keep your work very light.)

Remember there are many other ways and methods to make drawings. This book shows just one method. Why don't you seek out other ways from teachers, from libraries, and most importantly . . . from inside yourself?

Lee J. Ames

ANIMAL ART

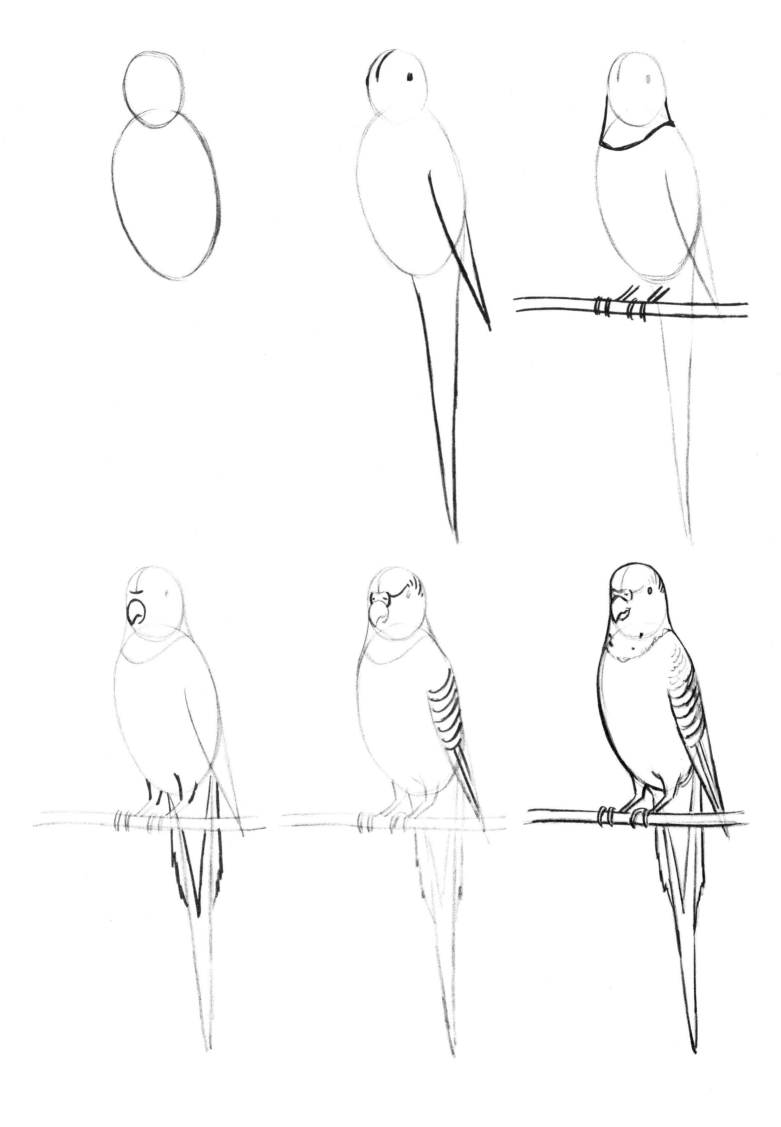

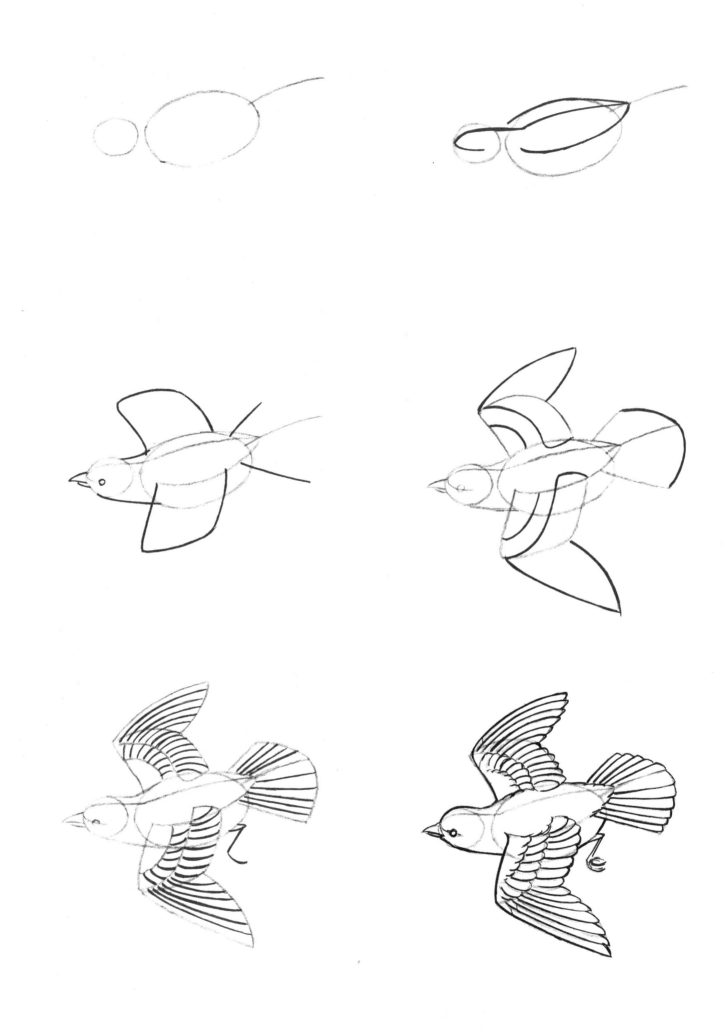

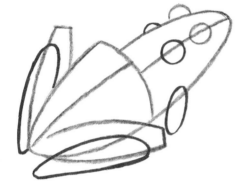

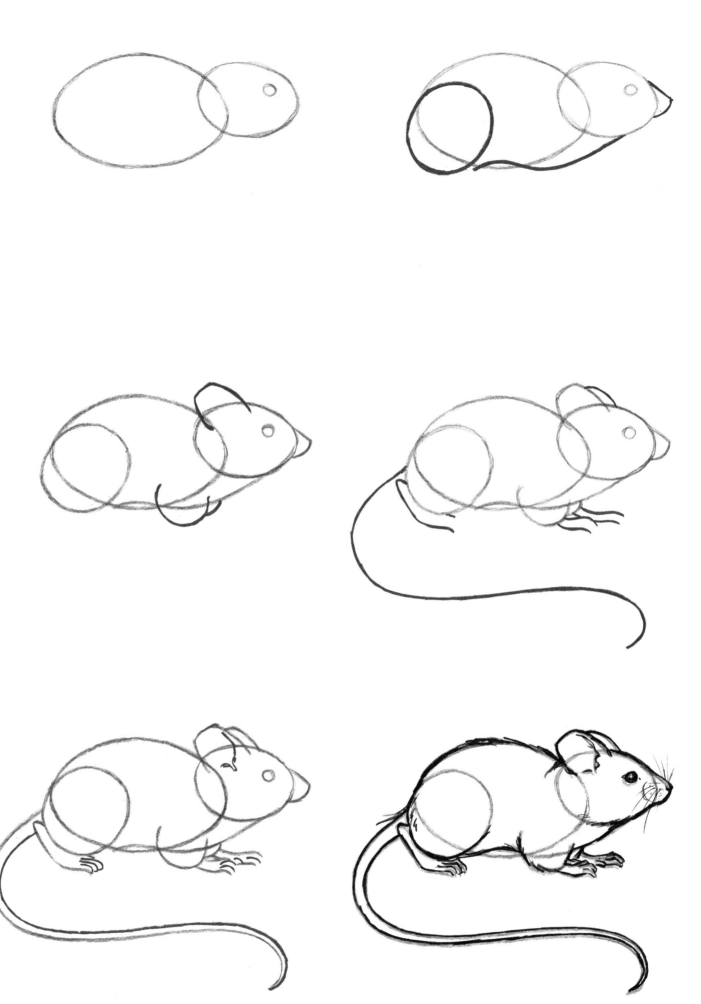

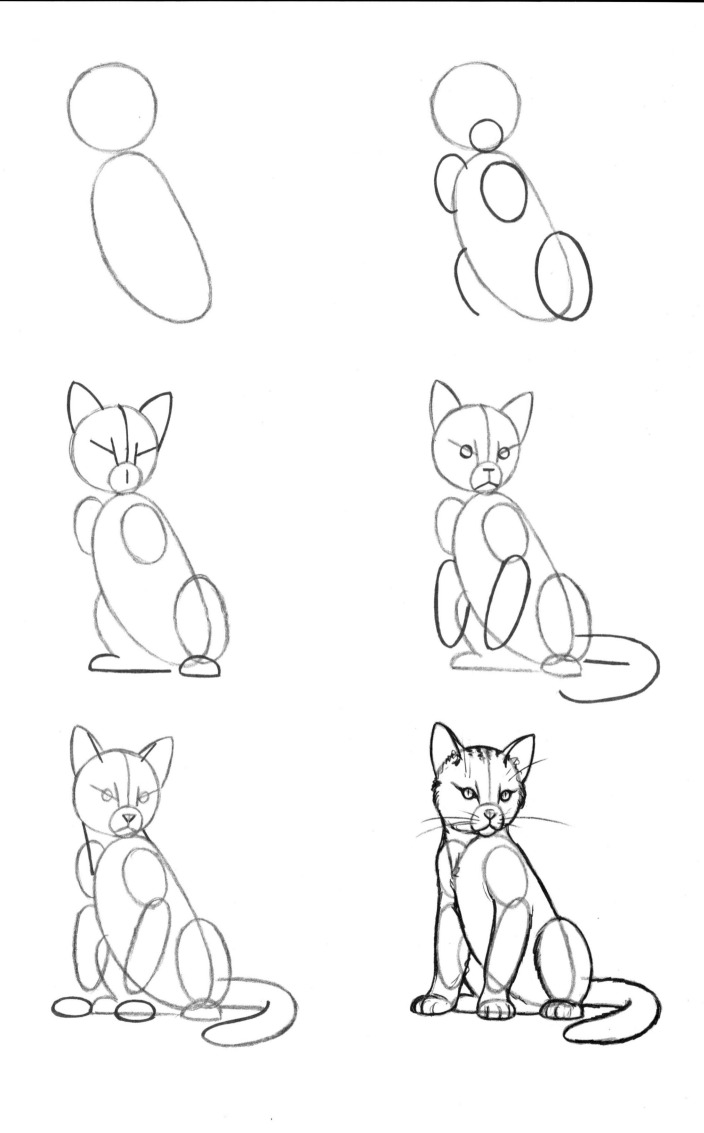

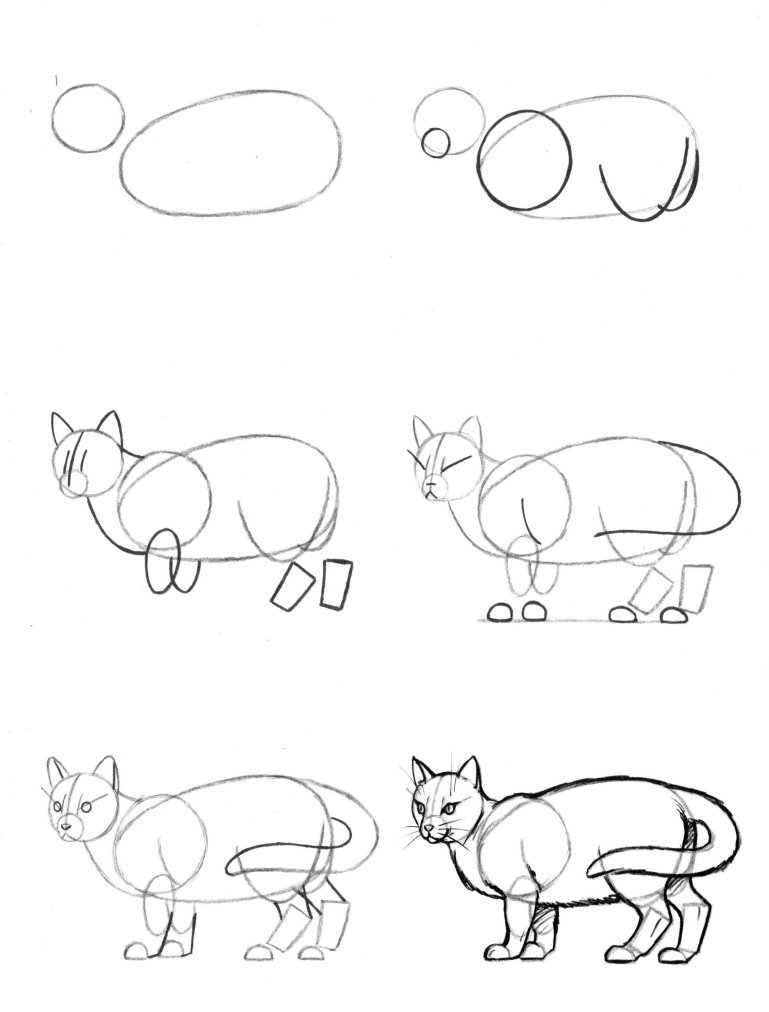

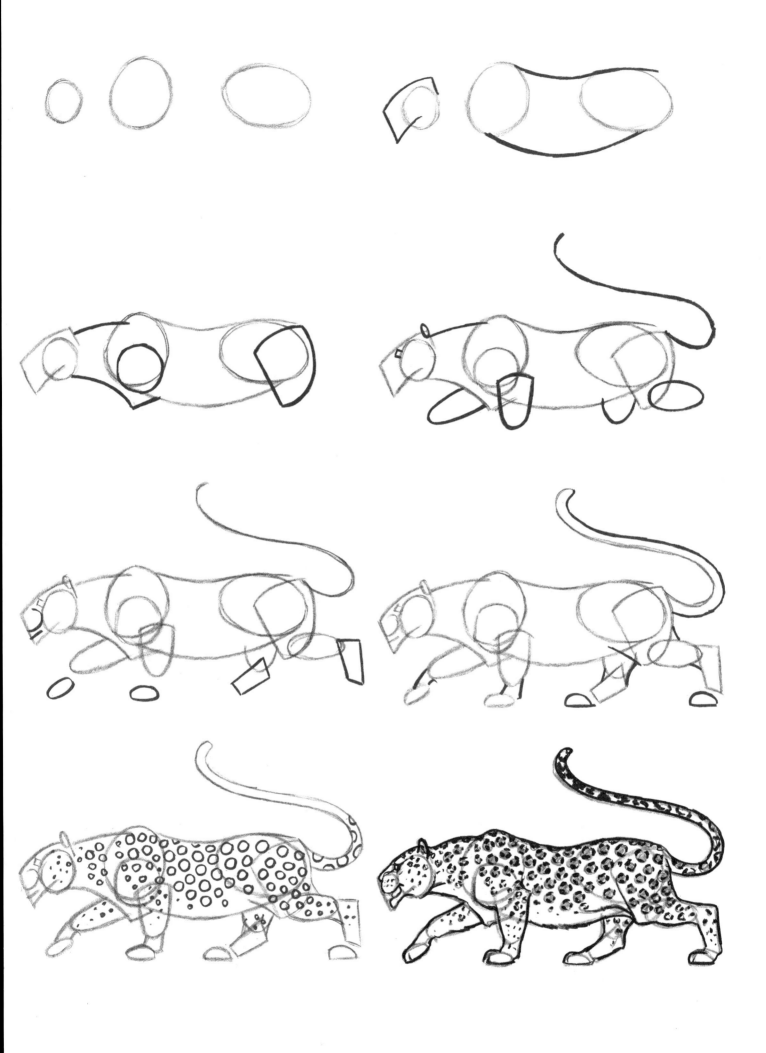

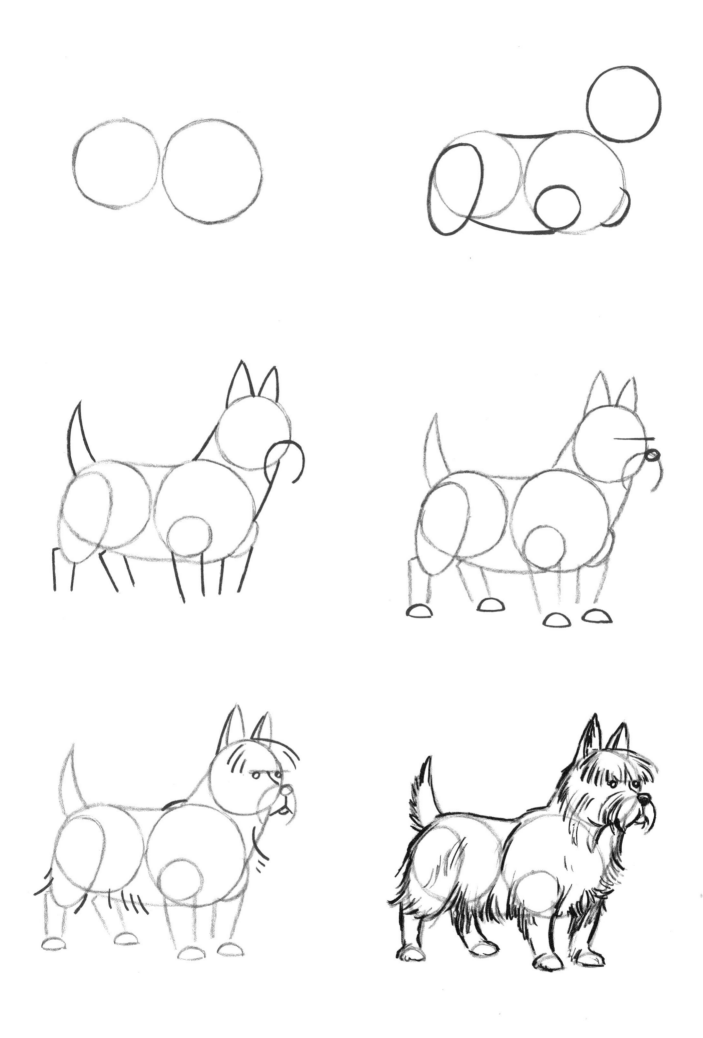

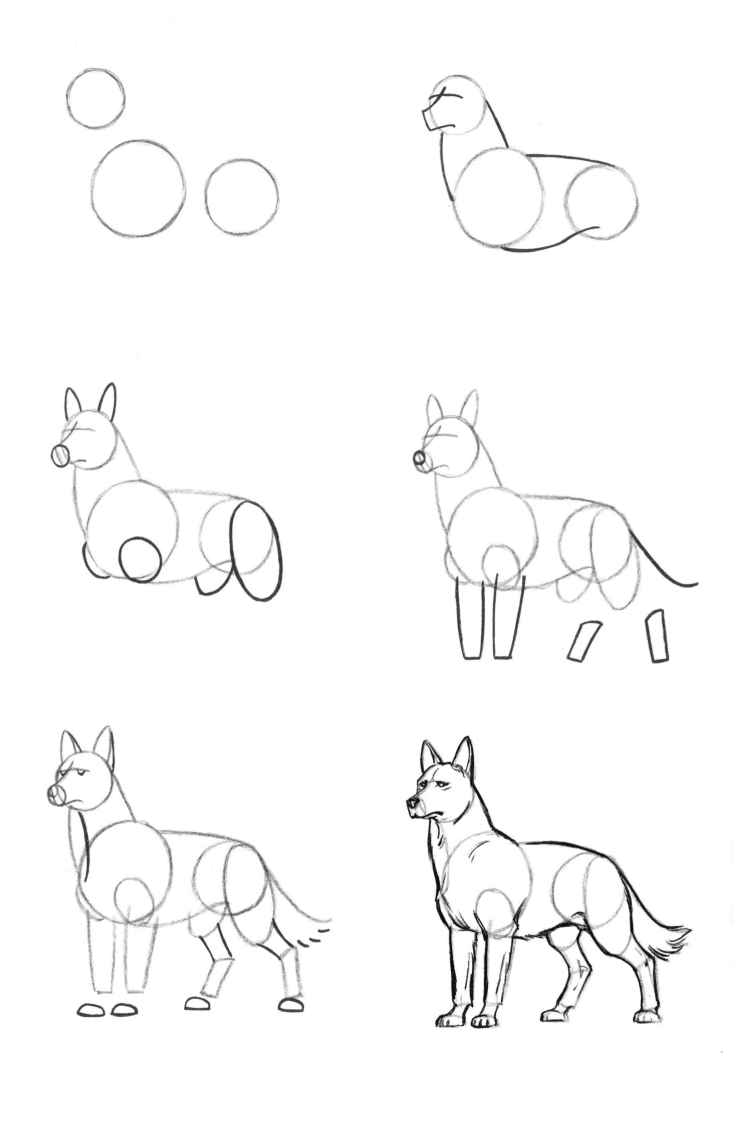

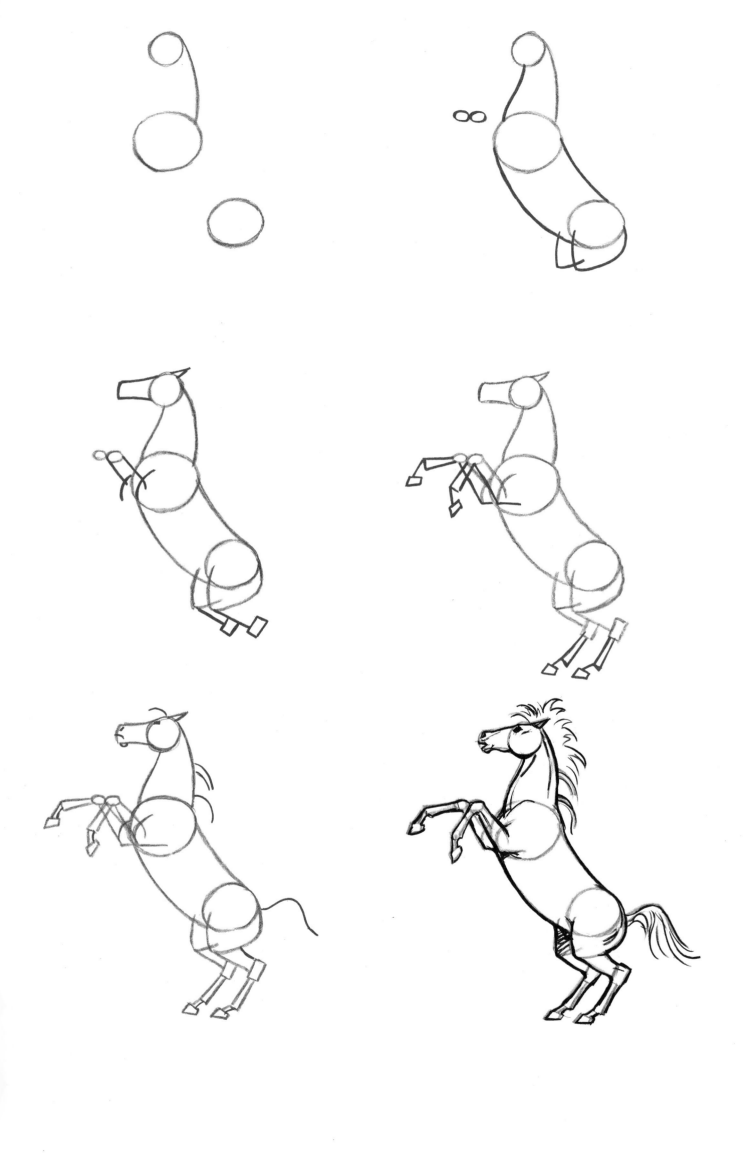

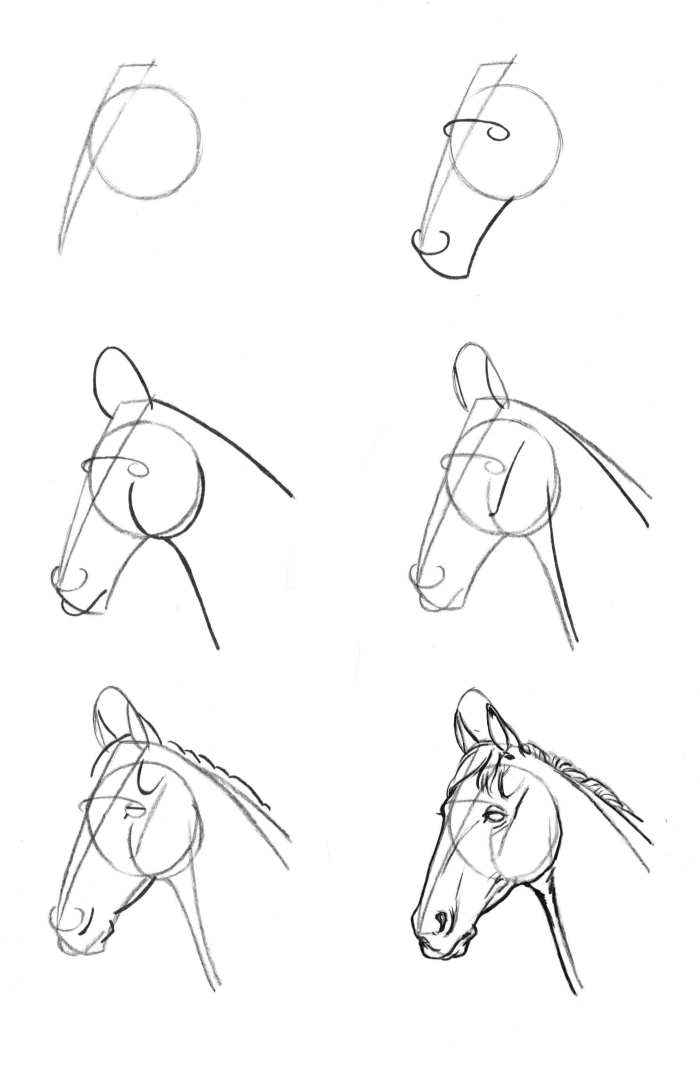

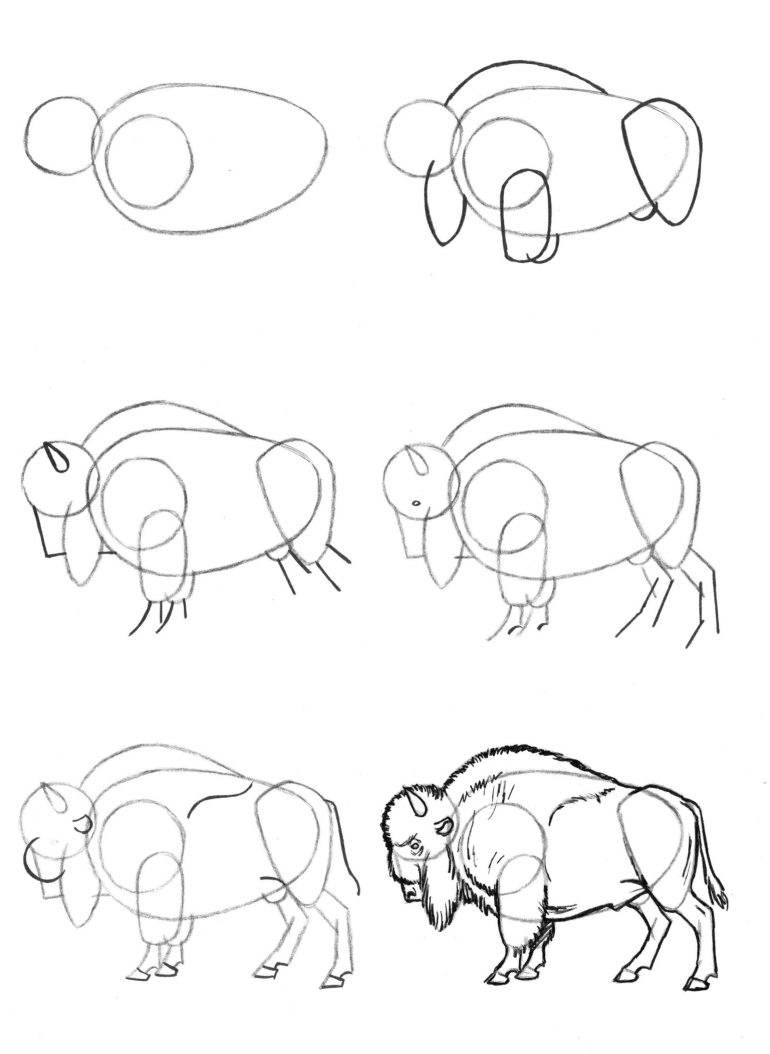

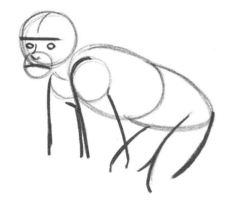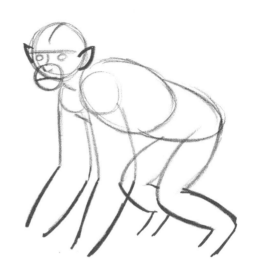

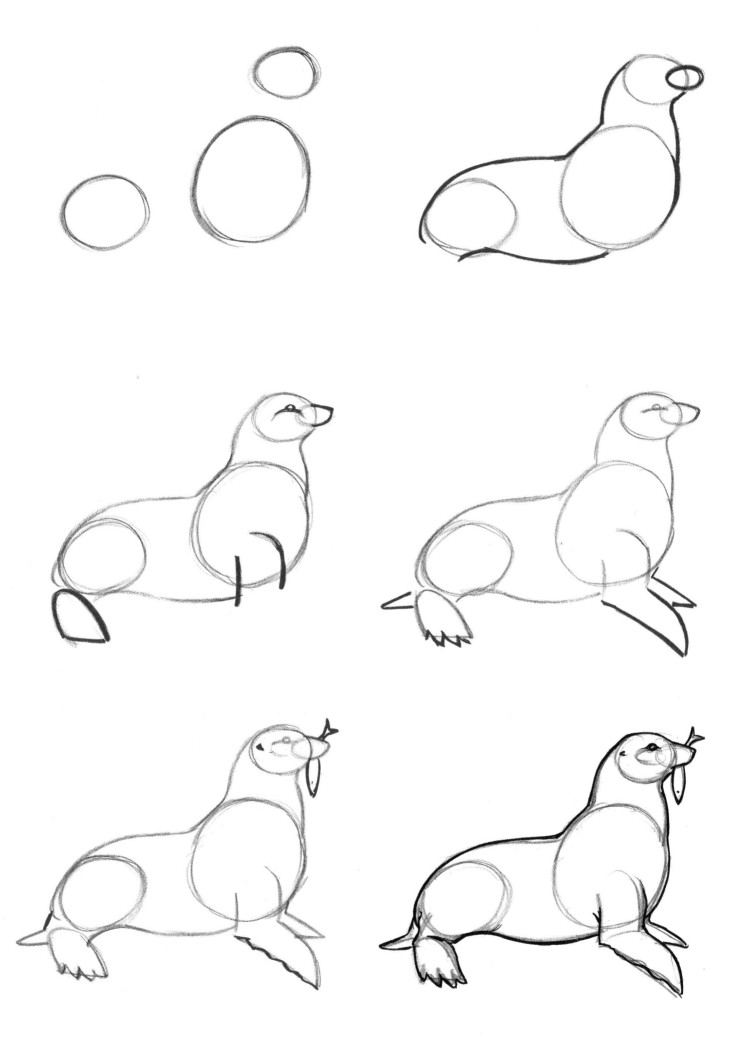

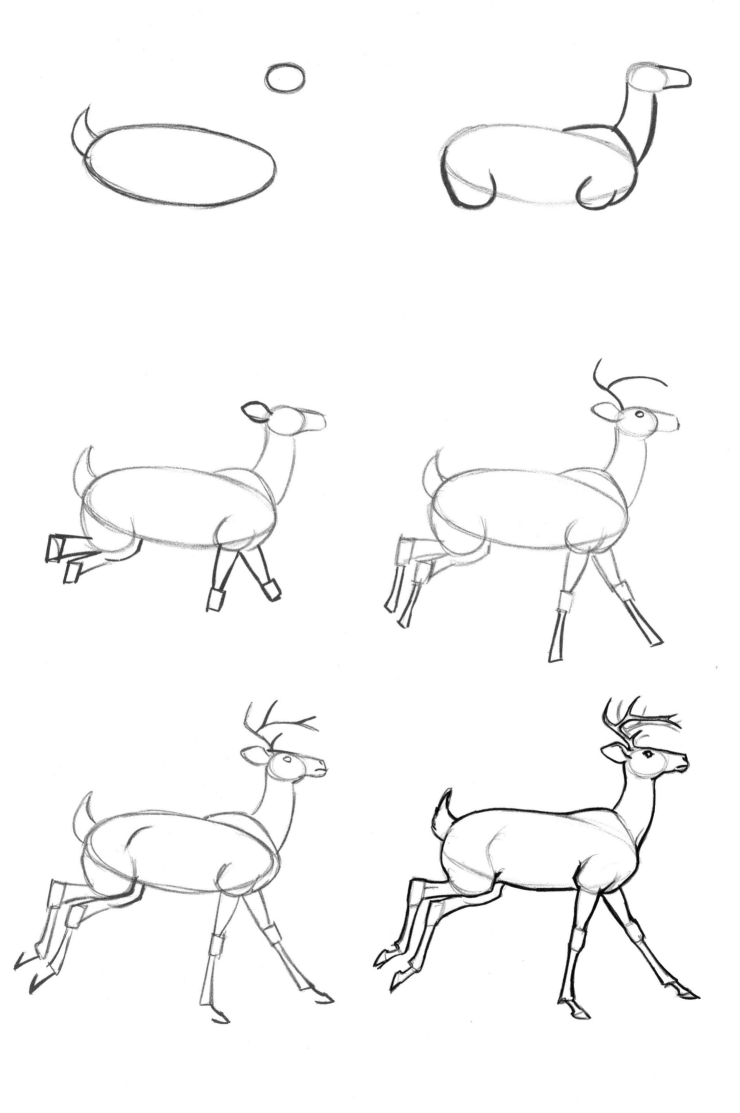

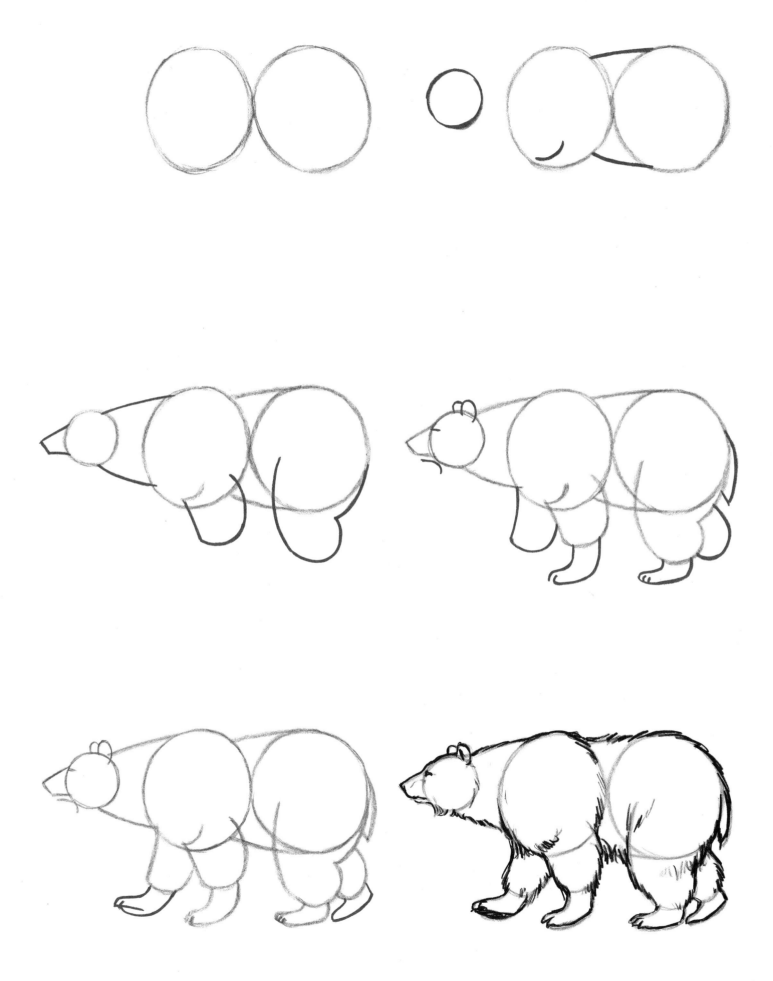

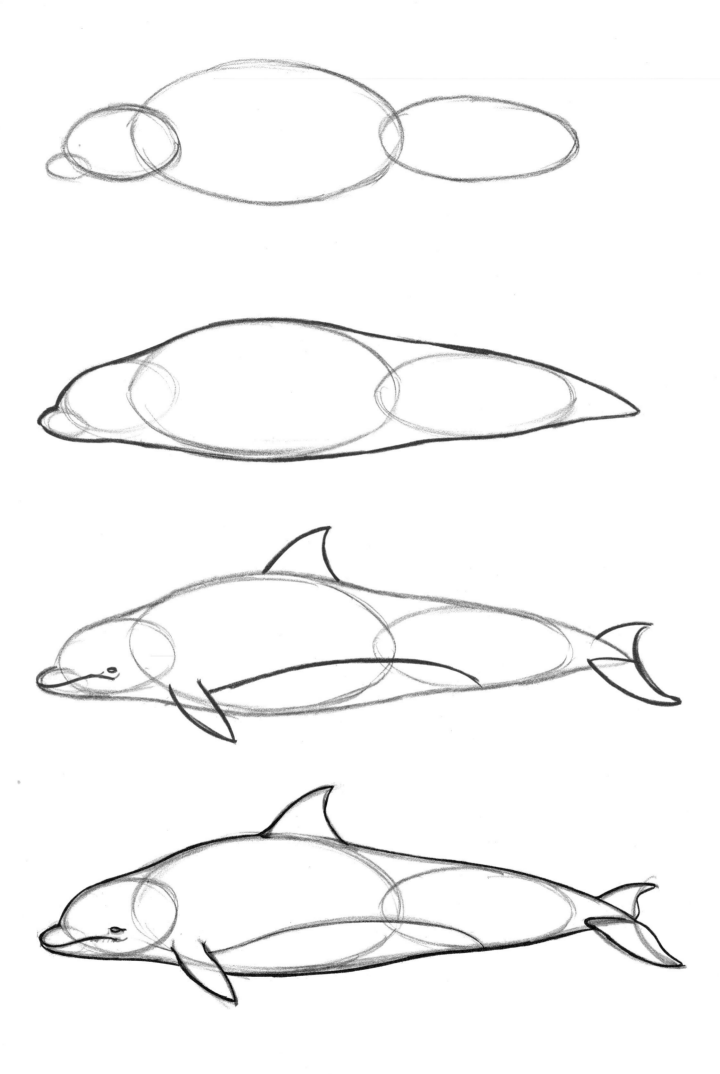

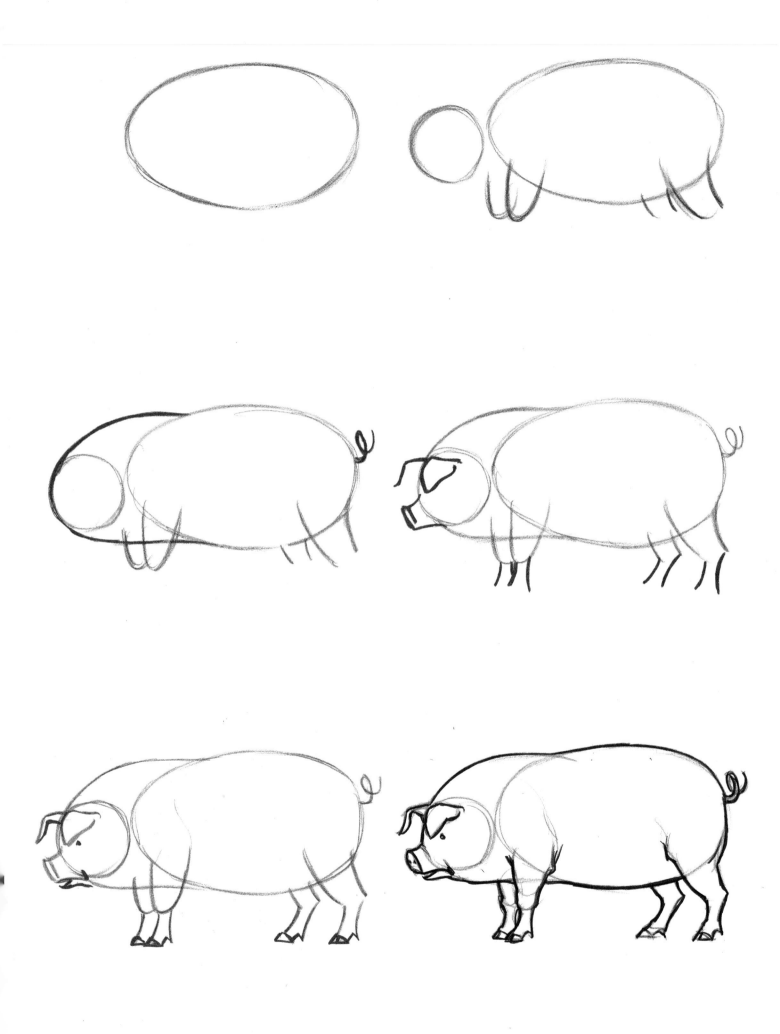

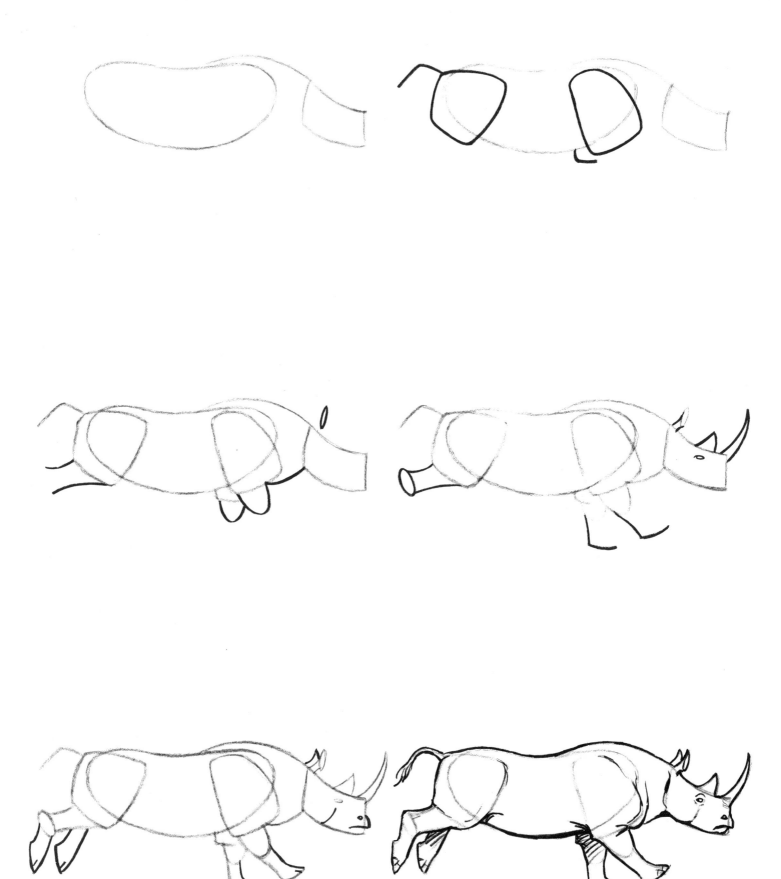

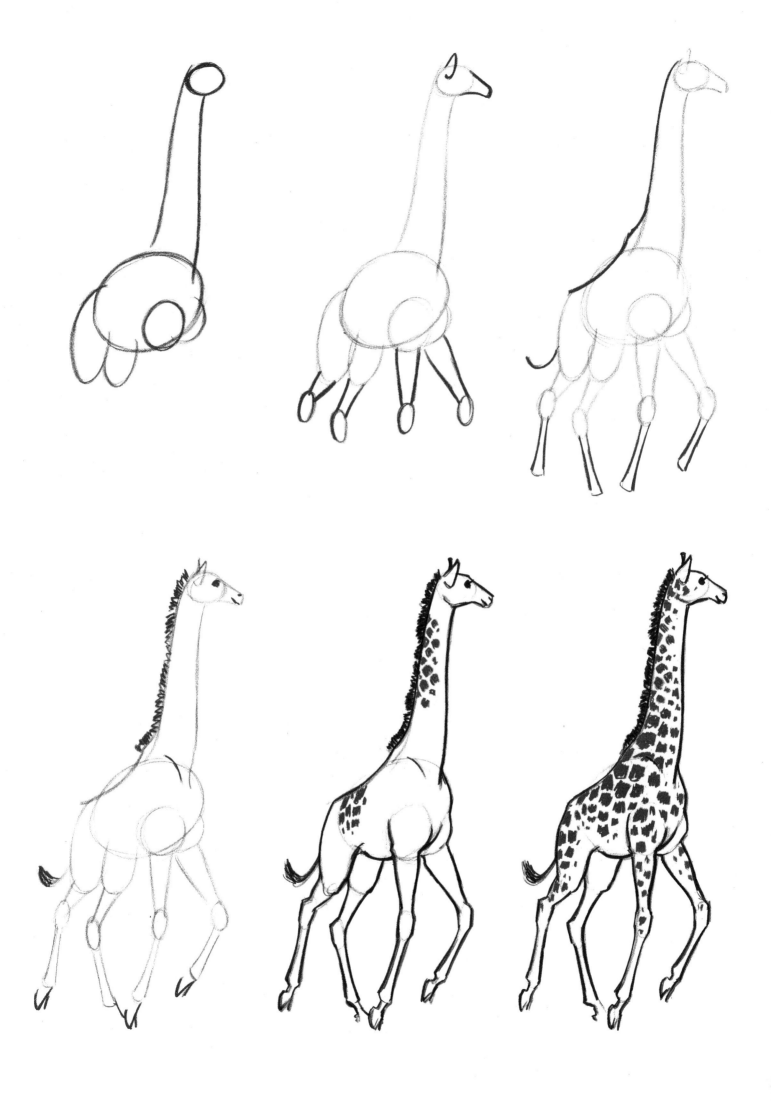

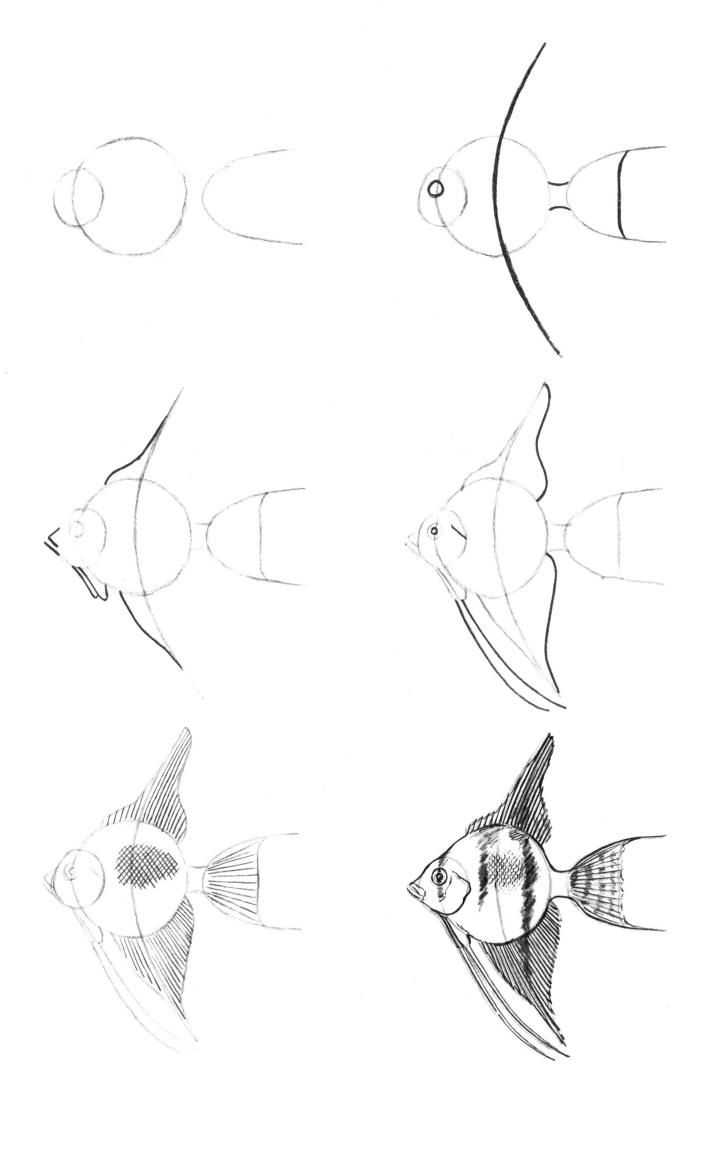

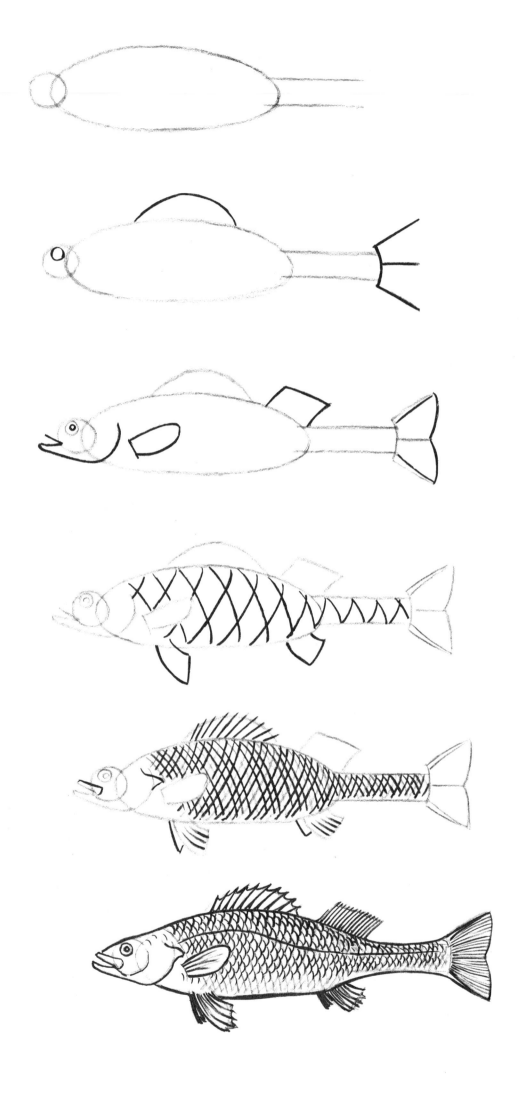

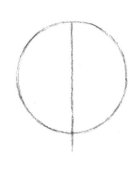
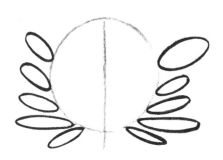
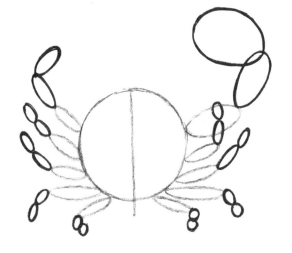
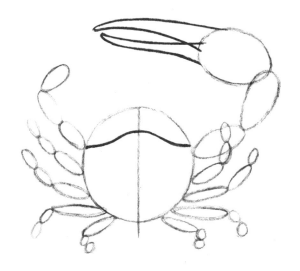

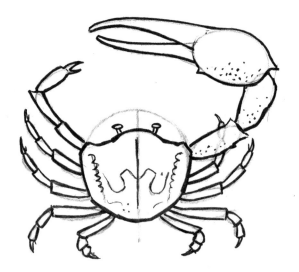

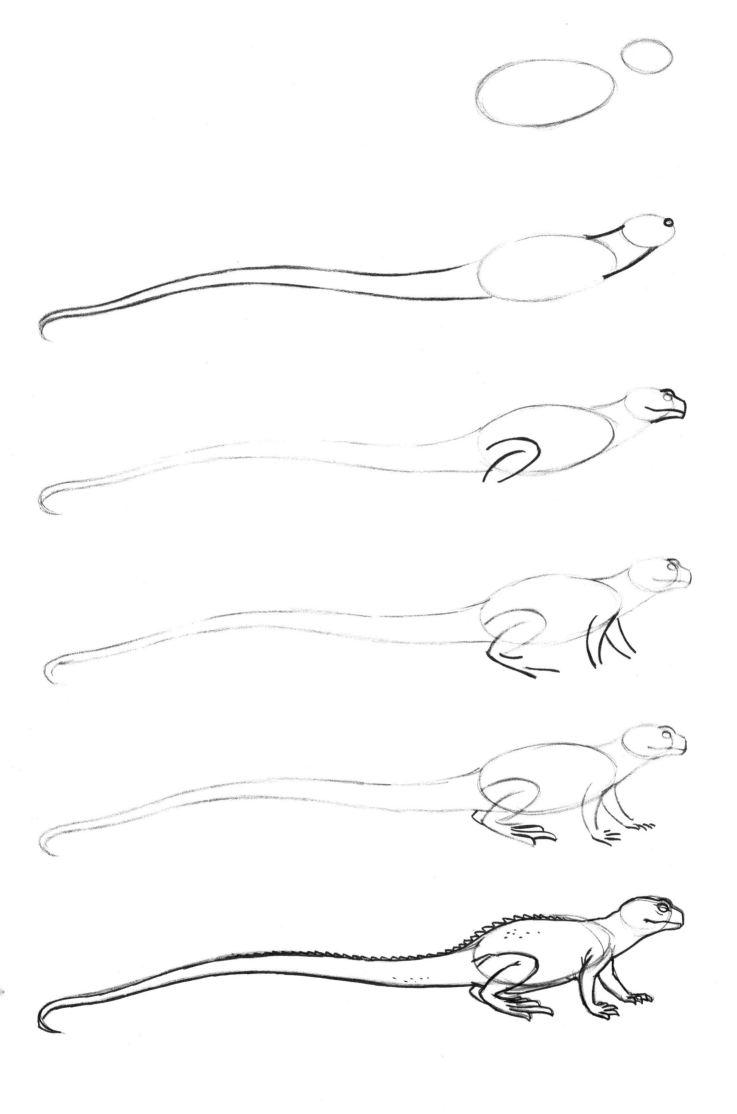

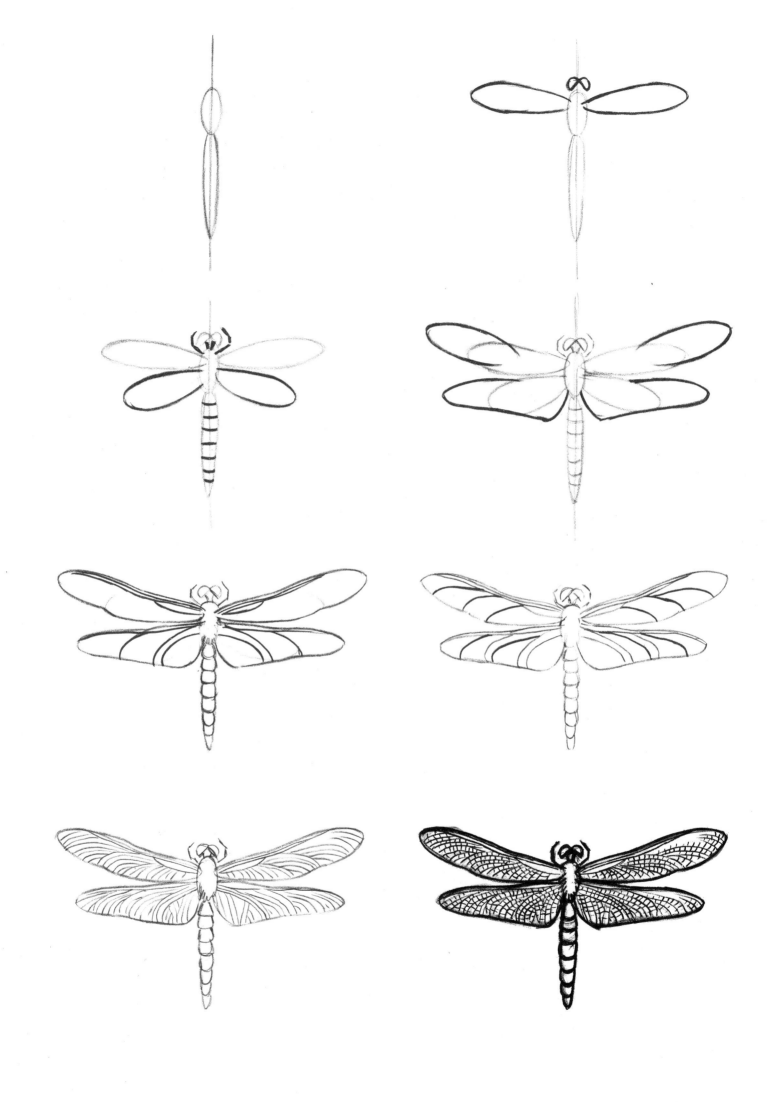

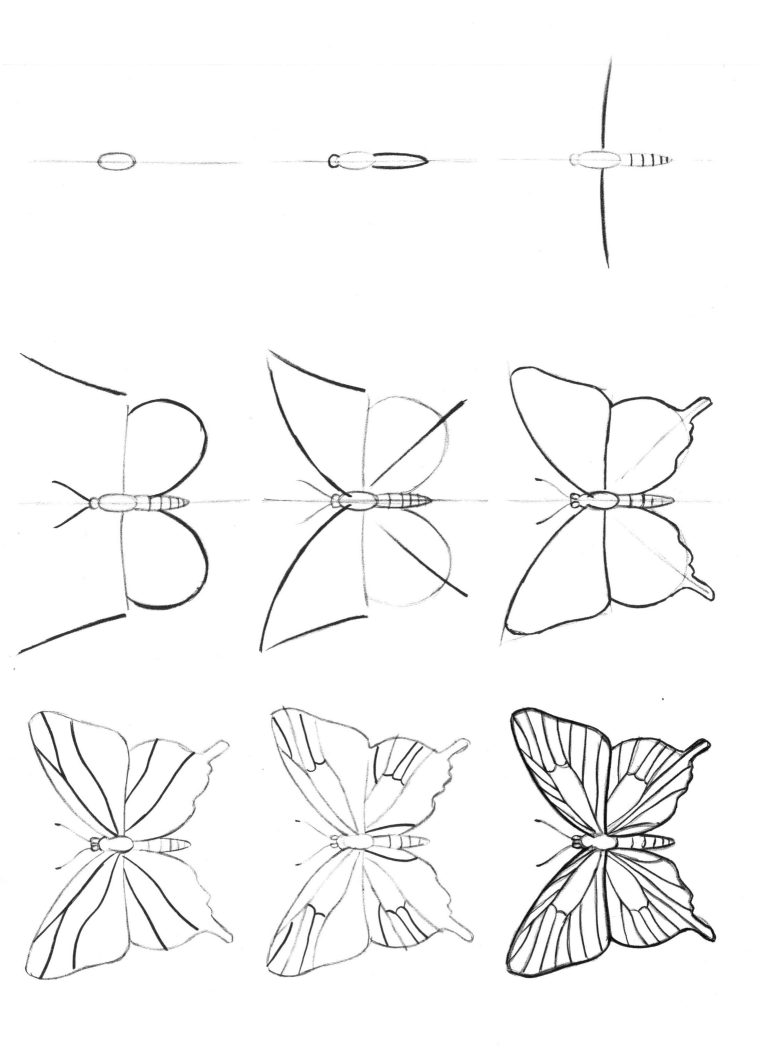

Lee J. Ames, a native New Yorker, has been earning his living as an artist for thirty-five years. He started out working on Walt Disney's *Fantasia* and *Pinocchio* in, what he himself describes as, a minimal capacity. He has also taught at the School of Visual Arts and, more recently, at Dowling College on Long Island. He owned and operated an advertising agency briefly and has done illustrations for several magazines. When not working, he enjoys tennis, maintaining a vegetable garden, and relaxing with his three cairn terriers Alfie, Betsy, and Cricket. Mr. Ames has illustrated over one hundred books, from preschool picture books to postgraduate texts.